MW00508948

Heart to Heart

Volume 1

A Collection of 24
Original, Inspirational,
and Spiritual Poems

Reginald O. Holden

TEACH Services, Inc.
P U B L I S H I N G
www.TEACHServices.com • (800) 367-1844

Copyright © 2015 Reginald O. Holden
Copyright © 2015 TEACH Services, Inc.
ISBN-13: 978-1-4796-0522-4 (Paperback)
ISBN-13: 978-1-4796-0526-2 (ePub)
ISBN-13: 978-1-4796-0530-9 (Mobi)
Library of Congress Control Number: 2015914768

All scripture quotations, unless otherwise indicated, are taken from the King James Version. Public domain.

TEACH Services, Inc.
P U B L I S H I N G
www.TEACHServices.com • (800) 367-1844

To my Lord and Savior, Jesus Christ,
To the memory of my mother and brother,
And to my family.

"A new heart also will I give you,
And a new spirit will I put within you:
And I will take away the stony heart out of your flesh,
And I will give you an heart of flesh."

Ezekiel 36:26

ABOUT THE BOOK

*H*eart to Heart, Volume 1, a collection
of 24 Unique, Inspirational, and Spiritual Poems,
is intended to encourage and motivate
The reader to a fuller and deeper relationship
with God, and his fellow man. It seeks
to highlight the importance of the real
and true Source—Jesus Christ—of strength
and happiness in dealing and coping with
life's hurts, disappointments, frustrations,
and in finding forgiveness, healing, joy,
and restoration through a loving-faith
relationship with Him. Only then will
we find purpose, meaning, and fulfillment
in our lives, our families, and other people
even in the midst of the trials, triumphs,
and sorrows of life.

INTRODUCTION

*H*ow do we find forgiveness, help, healing, peace,
and strength in the midst of life's storms, in the
midst of changing circumstances and times? How
do we keep from drowning in our problems,
and going under when the daily struggles and
pressures of life seem more than we can handle?
And how do we maintain a viable and vibrant
relationship with God, our family, our friends,
and other people? In these, and other questions,
Heart to Heart, Volume 1, in the imagery, music,
and muse of poetry, delves, and challenges us
to ponder, and to rise higher and still higher
in the journey of Christian growth towards
spiritual maturity.

The author

CONTENTS

COPING WITH LIFE

WHATEVER BETIDES...

*S*ometimes life's trials rush in like raging tides,
And you're beset by troubled waters on all sides.
When your hopes are dashed by the waves of doubt and fear,
And your dreams are shattered on the rocky pier,
Don't get discouraged by the boat you're in,
Trust in God when your back is against the wind.

Ah, toil, if you must, through rain or storm or stress,
But keep on rowing until you rise above the crest.
With a song on your lips and a prayer in your heart,
Exert every effort to strive for the mark.
Through tempest and gale you're destined to sail,
Yet trusting in God, you'll finally prevail!

When the journey is long and your faith gets low,
Stay the course; be steady as you go!
Endure each trial as you travel life's trip.
Take courage in peril but never abandon the ship.
So be faithful to your post for there's a victor's rest,
Whatever betides, trust in God 'til you're home with the blest!

"For whatsoever is born of God
Overcometh the world: And this is
The victory that overcometh the world,
Even our faith."

1 John 5:4

ONE MORE DAY
(A Christian Soldier's Challenge-1)

*O*ne more day to fight life's battles...
To war while there's still time—
'Tis no time now for discouragement,
For you've almost reached the finish line.

One more day to be courageous...
To stand up for the right,
Though the odds may be against you,
With Christ, you can win the fight.

One more day to hold on...
To endure when the wait seems long;
So bear every trial with patience,
For truth will soon triumph over wrong.

One more day to be faithful...
To work, watch, and pray,
To live the Christian Charter,
While helping others along life's way.

One more day to be victorious...
To overcome every fault and sin;
A soldier bravely fighting the warfare,
For there's a crown for you to win.

" Take unto you the whole
Armour of God, that ye may be able to
Withstand in the evil day,
And having done all,
To stand."

Ephesians 6:13

LORD, YOU KNOW ALL ABOUT IT...

Lord, You know all about it,
When things are going fine,
When I'm soaring like an eagle,
So high above the pines.

You know all about it,
When trouble comes my way,
When clouds are on the horizon,
The sky turns dark and gray.

You know all about it,
When others treat me wrong,
When I'm fighting life's hard battles,
I'll sing a happy song!

You know all about it,
When my faith is tested so,
When I'm flying through times of turbulence,
Your hand I won't let go.

You know all about it,
When I suffer misfortune or pain,
When the outlook gets a little cloudy,
Remember the bow comes after the rain.

You know all about it,
When my mind is stayed on You,
When I think of your wonderful promises…,
I know I will break through!

Lord, You know all about it,
So I'll rest in Your loving care,
For everything is in Your keeping,
Just like the lofty eagle so fair.

"But they that wait upon the LORD
Shall renew their strength; they shall
Mount up with wings as eagles:
They shall run, and not be weary;
And they shall walk, and
Not faint."

Isaiah 40:31

WEATHER THE WEATHER...

Life is like the weather...
Some days are good and bad.
Some make you lonely or sad.
Others bring lots of sunshine.
Some you're feeling just fine!
Some are gray and dreary.
Others you feel down and weary.
Some are blue and clear.
Some bring you laughter and cheer.
Others bring thunder, clouds and rain.
Some you have heartaches and pain.
Some are terrible and severe.
Others bring tornados, hurricanes, and fear.
Some have sleet and ice.
Some you just don't feel too nice.
Others bring lots of snow.
Some come with a rainbow.
Some you're floating like a feather.
But whatever...
Weather the weather...

"I can do all things through Christ
Which strengtheneth me."

Philippians 4:13

A BETTER COUNTRY

This old world is not my home,
For there's a better land I know;
So perfect, pure, and beautiful;
Where peace, joy, and eternal blessings flow!

No more trials and temptations;
No tempter to hurt or kill;
No sickness, pain, and suffering;
Not one will say, "I'm ill."

No more care, worry, and sorrow;
No sadness, guilt, or fear;
No sighing, crying, and weeping;
For Jesus will dry all tears.

No more death, sin, and sinners;
No strife, hatred, or war;
No fighting, killing, and dying;
All troubles will be o'er!

Yes, this old world will pass away,
For the Bible tells me so;
But my home is in an "heavenly country"
Where Jesus dwells I long to go!

"But now they desire a better country,
That is, an heavenly: wherefore
God is not ashamed to be called
Their God; for He hath
Prepared for them
A city."

Hebrews 11:16

SPIRITUAL HEALING AND GROWTH

CHARACTER

Like ancient builders of a mighty pyramid, tower or wall,
We, too, are builders of a great house, either crooked or tall.
Not a house made of mortar, brick, wood, or stone,
But of character, heart, soul, flesh, and bone.
Everyday we're building on solid rock or shifting sand,
A house that will finally fall or forever stand.

To build a strong and beautiful character is no easy feat;
For there are hard battles to fight and challenges to meet—
Test, trials and temptations both without and within;
The conquest of self, pride, guilt, fear, and sin.
Yet, with every successful step some progress is made;
For a sound character must be built upon a solid
foundation laid.

We are the architects of our own fate.
The master builders of the house we make;
For every motive, thought, and word is either right or wrong;
Every decision and deed forms a character either weak
or strong.
A house built on the shifting sand is never secure,
But the character built upon the solid Rock will forever endure

"For other foundation can no man lay than
That is laid, which is Jesus Christ."

1 Corinthians 3:11

A PRAYER FOR GRACE

Give me grace, Dear Lord, for this day anew…
Grace to reflect the image of You.

Grace to hear the Spirit's quiet voice.
Grace to be thankful, sing and rejoice!

Grace to walk in all Your ways…
Grace to always give You the praise…

Grace to love You with all my heart, soul and mind.
Grace to let my light shine!

Grace for each moment the whole day through…
Grace to reflect the image of You!

Amen

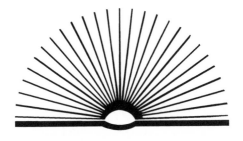

"But we all, with open face beholding
As in a glass the glory of the Lord,
Are changed into the same image
From glory to glory, even as by
The Spirit of the Lord."

2 Corinthians 3:18

OH GRACE SUFFICIENT

Oh grace sufficient so rich and free;
Jesus died for a sinner like me.
His sinless life He gave for mine;
My salvation He purchased by love divine.
He paid the ransom with His own perfect life;
The Son of God became the Lamb of sacrifice.
His precious blood for me was shed;
On Calvary's Cross for my sins He bled!

Oh grace sufficient so just and true;
Jesus transforms my nature anew.
His holy life to me He imparts;
My will I surrender for a clean heart.
The guilt of my past He freely forgives;
Through faith in Christ, the Law of God I live.
He sends the Holy Spirit like a rushing wind;
By His indwelling power I overcome sin!

Oh grace sufficient so humble and meek;
Jesus lives for the sinner to seek.
Himself He gave to set us free;
Our salvation He brought for eternity...
He paid the ransom with His own perfect life;
The Son of God became the Lamb of sacrifice.
His precious blood for us was shed;
On Calvary's Cross for our sins He bled!

"...Behold the Lamb of God, which taketh
Away the sin of the world."

John 1:29

FORGIVE ME PRAYER

Forgive me Lord, for breaking Your heart,
When You died for me at Calvary.
You suffered so much on that cruel cross;
So much guilt, pain, and agony.

Forgive me Lord, for causing Your guilt,
When You bore all my sin and shame.
I should have been on that cruel cross,
But instead You took the blame.

Forgive me Lord, for causing Your pain,
When they nailed You to the tree.
I should have been on that cruel cross,
But You died that I might be free.

Forgive me Lord, for causing Your agony,
When You couldn't see Your Father's face.
I should have been on that cruel cross,
But You chose to take my place.

Forgive me Lord, for breaking Your heart,
When You died for me at Calvary.
You suffered so much on that cruel cross;
O may I see how great is Your love for me!

Amen

"But God commendeth His love toward us,
In that, while we were yet sinners,
Christ died for us."

Romans 5:8

A TIME TO REST

A time to work...
A time to rest...
A time to worship...
A time to be blest...

Six days of the week
God made for labor;
For man to work
Like his Lord and Creator.

One day of the week
God made for rest;
For man to remember
The Sabbath Day He blest.

The seventh day of the week
God made for worship;
To praise and honor Him
For His wonderful works...

A time to work...
A time to rest...
A time to worship...
A time to be blest...

"Remember the Sabbath day,
To keep it holy."

Exodus 20:8

THE LORD'S DAY

*I*t is Friday evening.
The sun is setting behind the western horizon,
As night etches the sky with clouds of kaleidoscopic hue.
Unlike any other day—from sunset to sunset,
This is the Lord's Day; a sacred day; the seventh day.
God has finished His glorious work;
The grand and awe-inspiring work of creation in six days.
He rested (as if God needed to rest).
He rested not as a tried and exhausted man,
But as the Creator-God.
He rested because His work was indeed good…
Man was good;
Everything was good—animate and inanimate.

And so all men are enjoined everywhere to rest
From his work (as the Creator rested from His);
To give glory, honor, praise, and worship
To the Creator-God of the Universe
On The Lord's Day—The Sabbath.

"But the seventh day is the Sabbath
Of the LORD thy God..."

Exodus 20:10

TEACH ME PRAYER

*T*each me Lord, to wait on You,
When I cannot see the way,
When darkness hides Your face from view,
Give me light to see Your will today.

Teach me Lord, to rest in You,
When I am burdened with care and sorrow.
Grant me the peace that passes understanding,
When I pass through the storms of tomorrow.

Teach me Lord, to trust in You,
When I would faint with doubt and tears.
Give me grace to understand the wisdom
And blessing of each new trial without fears.

Teach me Lord, to walk with You,
Through darkness, storm or trial.
Until, at last, I see Your face
And behold Your loving smile.

Amen

"Show me thy ways, O LORD;
Teach me thy paths."

Psalm 25:4

FLY...

*H*igher and higher;
On the wings of destiny fly...
Higher and higher;
Like an eagle in the sky.

Higher and higher;
Through faith begin.
Higher and higher;
With every round ascend.

Higher and higher;
To valor and virtue.
Higher and higher;
In knowledge, wisdom, truth and statute.

Higher and higher;
On the wings of destiny fly...
Higher and higher;
Like an eagle in the sky.

Higher and higher;
Through discipline and obedience.
Higher and higher;
With perseverance and patience.

Higher and higher;
In service, kindness and duty.
Higher and higher;
From godliness to charity.

Higher and higher;
On the wings of destiny fly...
Higher and higher still;
From glory to glory...

"And now abideth faith, hope, and charity,
These three; but the greatest of these is
Charity."

1 Corinthians 13:13

FRIENDSHIP

PEOPLE LIKE YOU

*I*t isn't very often to find people like you;
Maybe one-in-a-million, maybe two!
People who show by word and deed,
Just what it means to help others in need.

We all need a helping hand along life's way;
A gentle touch, a kind word, who can say?
It takes a special person to go the extra mile;
To lift the load, to persevere under trial.

While others merely boast but never really share,
Still you show from the heart your love and care.
Now the world's a better place because you say and
Do.
O how I wish there were more people just like you!

"A man that hath friends
Must show himself friendly:
And there is a friend that sticketh
Closer than a brother."

Proverbs 18:24

PLEASE FORGIVE ME

Sometimes we speak unkind words...
Or offend people by what we do...
But do we ever say, "I'm sorry",
Or "please forgive me for hurting you"?

We all need forgiveness —
To be forgiven and to forgive...
Though we've made mistakes and hurt people,
When we forgive ourselves and others, we live...

Life's just too short to hold a grudge;
To go on hating, hurting, and shoving...
But there's a better way — God's healing way;
To experience the healing power of forgiving and loving...

"For if ye forgive men their trepasses,
Your heavenly Father will also
Forgive you…"

Matthew 6:14

THE LITTLE THINGS MATTER

*I*t's the little things that matter
That make our lives sweeter.
It's a kind and gentle heart of giving
That makes life worth living!

There's a mystical power in what we say;
For gracious words have influence to sway.
Hello, good morning, and how do you do?
Please or thank you or I love you?

But sharp words and verbal attacks...
Are like a cold shoulder or a stab-in-the-back.
Once uttered they never are recalled.
Such words should never be spoken at all!

With a handshake or hug or a friendly kiss,
We can bring others sweetness and bliss.
We hold the keys to our own plight...
By whether we treat others with kindness or slight.

"…If any man offend not in word,
The same is a perfect man,
And able also to bridle
The whole body."

James 3:2

MY FAITHFUL FRIEND

Who is a friend like Jesus? So faithful, kind and true;
A Friend above all others, He gave His life for you!

He will never fail you. He'll always be the same.
Though friends may often falter, His love will never change.

He's closer than a brother; He's an ever-abiding Friend.
Someone you can rely on; He'll be there until the end.

He listens when you call Him. Your faintest prayer He hears.
You're always in His heart. His presence is ever near.

He'll never leave you in trouble, but stay right by your side.
Through every valley or mountain, He'll be your faithful
Guide.

He knows about your heartaches; each trial and each care.
His arms of love are outstretched. Your burdens He will bear.

You can safely trust Him to supply your every need...
For there's no friend like Jesus, my faithful Friend indeed!

"…I will never leave thee,
Nor forsake thee."

Hebrews 13:5

LOVE AND HAPPINESS

I LOVE YOU

I love you with all my heart,
For each day throughout the year.
No matter the weather or season,
On cloudy days or clear.

I love you for a million reasons...
For all the things you do;
For being my faithful partner,
To share life's journey as two.

I love you for how you cope,
When our plans don't turn out right,
When our hopes and dreams elude us,
Or when the money gets a little tight.

I love you the way you are;
For the woman you've come to be.
You're the one I love to be with...
You're that special person for me.

But most of all I love you,
Because you love me so,
And of all the many reasons,
That's the greatest one I know!

"The heart of her husband
Doth safely trust in her,
So that he shall have
No need of spoil."

Proverbs 31:11

YOU MEAN SO MUCH

You mean so much to me,
Dear sweetheart, friend and wife.
You're that one special person;
The woman I chose for life.

You mean so much to me.
A friend right from the start,
To share my hopes and dreams—
The secrets of my heart.

You mean so much to me.
I love to have you near.
Your words are kind and gracious.
Your smile gives warmth and cheer.

You mean so much to me,
To have you by my side,
To live and laugh together,
Through trust in God abide!

You mean so much to me
With each new and passing day,
Though the years may come and go,
My love for you will always stay!

"…This is now bone of my bones,
And flesh of my flesh…"

Genesis 2:23

MY SPECIAL LADY

*Y*ou are my special lady, like a rare diamond so fine.
The woman of my heart desires, my favorite valentine.

My wife and helpmate, a dream come true.
My friend and sweetheart; honey, I love you.

God put you by my side to walk and work together;
To love each other through any kind of weather.

You are my special lady, the apple of my eye.
Far beyond the price of rubies, your worth money can't buy.

I see your outer beauty, your many virtues too;
Kindness, grace, and compassion are just a few!

Our lives are knit together in heaven's harmony;
Body, mind, and spirit in perfect unity.

You are my special lady, an integral part of me;
"Flesh of my flesh and bone of my bone"!

"Therefore shall a man leave his father and
His mother, and shall cleave unto his wife:
And they shall be one flesh."

Genesis 2:24

THANK YOU

*T*hank you for choosing me to share my life with you;
For giving me your heart when you said "I do."

Thank you for being my queen, my wife and lover-girl;
The mother of our children—God's gift of precious pearls!

Thank you for your kindness; for your warm and caring ways;
For living to bless others, a fitting tribute to Mother's Day!

Thank you for your laughter; for the radiance of your face;
For the joy of special moments-a kiss, a hug, or tender embrace.

Thank you for your love; for affection so fair and fond;
For the gift of friendship shared when two hearts bond.

Thank you for all you've done to make our house a home;
A place where peace abides, and God's grace is enthroned!

Thank you for choosing me to share my life with you;
'Tis the blessing of a life-time because I said, "I do."

"What therefore God hath joined together,
Let not man put asunder."

Mark 10:9

GOD'S LOVE

THE ROBIN'S NEST

Early in the morning,
One beautiful spring day,
I heard the birds sweetly singing—
The robin, sparrow, and blue jay.

As I peered through my window,
Such lovely birds I saw.
When suddenly came mother robin,
Bringing with her mud, feathers, and straw!

I watched in utter surprise,
As day after day she came,
To dwell in this quaint spot—
Right here in my windowpane.

From dawn to dust she toiled,
With undaunted zeal and zest,
Until her new home was finished.
O what a beautiful nest!

Soon she started her family,
And the little eggs came so quick.
Her nest was filled to overflowing,
No room for any more chicks.

Tenderly she cared for her young,
Watching them as they grew.
Then one by one they left her,
Perhaps they'll be mothers too!

Now the nest is empty.
The birds have all flown away.
But the lesson of mother robin's nest,
Bespeaks of my Father's love and care each day!

"Fear ye not therefore, ye are of more
Value than many sparrows."

Matthew 10:31

GOD'S CHILD

I have a heavenly Father,
Who's watching over me.
I know He's close by my side,
Though His face I cannot see.

When I behold the starry heavens…
And His handiwork in nature…,
I know He upholds all things…
And He holds my future…

So why should I worry?
I think awhile, and smile
And raise my eyes to heaven
And say, "I am God's child."

"And will be a Father unto you,
And ye shall be my sons and daughters,
Saith the Lord Almighty."

2 Corinthians 6:18

SMILE, GOD LOVES YOU

When life's trials are hard to bear,
And you feel discouraged and in despair,
When your friends all but forsake you,
And you just don't know what to do,
Don't let trials or people get you down,
Or break your heart, or make you frown.

The game of life is not always fair.
But who's immune from trouble or care?
You remember Job's story, and his lot?
He kept the faith despite the enemy's plot.
You don't have to fret, worry or doubt.
Everything's in God's hand so why pout?

Sooner or later the trials will abate.
Your blessing will come; for God's never late.
Hold on a little longer and wait and see
How the cares you bear, He'll make them to flee.
So don't get discouraged in trials you're going through...
Just smile, and remember that God loves you!

"They that sow in tears shall reap in joy."

Psalm 126:5

"And I will put my Spirit within you,
And cause you to walk in my statues,
And ye shall keep my judgments,
And do them."

Ezekiel 36:27

Successful Strategies for Coping with Life!
How do you find forgiveness, help, healing, peace, and strength in
the midst of changing circumstances and times? How do you keep
from drowning in your problems, and going under when the daily
struggles and pressures of life seem more than you can handle?
Heart to Heart, Volume 1, seeks to encourage, motivate, and inspire
the reader to a fuller and deeper relationship with God, family, and
fellowman while dealing and coping with life's issues...
Only then will one find answers to life's deepest problems, questions,
purpose, meaning, and fulfillment in living...

Reginald O. Holden, born in 1952, is the third of five children.
He grew up in a God-fearing and Christian home in a small
rural town in Northwestern New Jersey. As a youngster,
his life was shaped and influenced by country living and the practi-
cal, biblical, and ethical principles that his parents sought to instill.
These values and lessons have been, and continue to be, *a vital and
motivating strength* in dealing with the challenges and vicissitudes
in his life. ***Heart to Heart, Volume 1***, is a glimpse in his heart—his
dreams, disappointments, fears, frustrations, hope, hurts, joys, trials,
and triumphs—and how he found help, healing, happiness, and
strength in his relationships with God, his family, and his fellowman.
Reginald writes from Alabama where he works, and resides with his
wife, best friend, and college sweetheart, Deloras. They have two
lovely and aspiring adult children, Letitia and Brian. He enjoys writ-
ing, reading, gardening, walking, playing and listening to classical
and spiritual piano music.

We invite you to view the complete
selection of titles we publish at:
www.TEACHServices.com

scan with your mobile
device to go directly
to our website

Please write or email us your praises, reactions, or
thoughts about this or any other book we publish at:

www.TEACHServices.com • (800) 367-1844

P.O. Box 954
Ringgold, GA 30736

Info@TEACHServices.com

TEACH Services, Inc., titles may be purchased in bulk for
educational, business, fund-raising, or sales promotional use.
For information, please e-mail:

BulkSales@TEACHServices.com

Finally if you are interested in seeing
your own book in print, please contact us at

publishing@TEACHServices.com

We would be happy to review your manuscript for free.

CPSIA information can be obtained
at www.ICGtesting.com
Printed in the USA
BVHW071417010619
549897BV00003B/222/P